THE PARISH HELP BOOK

A Guide to Social Ministry in the Parish

HERBERT F. WEBER

AVE MARIA PRESS Notre Dame, Indiana

International Standard Book Number: 0-87793-304-9

Library of Congress Catalog Card Number: 83-71894

Printed and bound in the United States of America.

Cover design: Katherine A. Robinson
Text design: Elizabeth French

THE PARISH HELP BOOK

TO MY MOTHER,
WHO TAUGHT ME COMPASSION;
TO MY FATHER,
WHO GUIDED ME IN JUSTICE.

CONTENTS

ACKNOWLEDGMENTS

Last year I was involved in conducting several workshops throughout our diocese to help parishes respond to the needs of the people in their communities. The turnout for the sessions was overwhelming. One common request from the participants was for something in writing that could guide their work. Thus the seeds were planted for what eventually developed into this book.

In a very true sense, then, these chapters were inspired by the very people to whom they are directed. Moreover, their inspiration for this work is also evident in that many of the vignettes and examples are the stories of their work.

Therefore, I extend my thanks to the men and women in our parishes who have exemplified the care and concern for those in need.

Also, thanks must be expressed to the staff of Catholic Charities of Chicago, where I was first introduced to parish social ministry several years ago.

Finally, in a special way, my appreciation is directed to the staff members of Catholic Social Services and the Office of Community Relations of the Toledo Diocese. Their support and assistance helped in a profound way. Two persons must be mentioned by name. One is Donna

Therkelsen, who helped with some research and advised me, especially with Chapter Six. The other is the director of Catholic Social Services, Father Robert Haas, who offered more than a few encouraging words along the way. Thanks to all.

—Herb Weber

INTRODUCTION

Two recent developments illustrate efforts by the church to be a church of charity and justice. One was the sudden sprouting of shelters for the homeless in parishes throughout the country; the second was the American bishops' statement on war and peace.

Concern for those who are most in need has always characterized the church or, at least, its ideals about itself. And specifically concern for the homeless can be traced back to Jesus' criteria for judgment, recorded in Matthew 25. The sudden and widespread concern for the homeless of our day, nonetheless, represents a recovery of basic charity that had all too often become the preserve of social-work professionals, government services, and specialized institutions. Parishes now reach out to provide the most basic of services to those most in need. And, if parish ministers have any thoughts that people did not care about others, the generous response by parishioners who were willing to give of their time and energy should dispel such misunderstanding.

But parish involvement in shelter for the homeless illustrates many other aspects of today's social ministry, besides the basic expression of charity. In many cities, parishes cooperate with city agencies. Often, the city provides the beds, screens the homeless and provides other support for voluntary efforts. On the other hand, in places like New York City, where the city has a legal obligation to provide shelter, the parishes assist the city in fulfilling its obligations.

Secondly, in addition to the collaboration of private and public institutions, the care for the homeless made many people aware of the numbers, conditions and sources of homeless in our society. Involvement in the service became the best education about the problem. People learned about the plight of the alcoholic, about the thousands of people wandering the streets after having been released from state mental hospitals, about the new homeless (especially whole families) who had lost their homes because they had lost their jobs, and about those set adrift because they cannot cope with the challenges of today's living.

Thirdly, care for the homeless led many church people into new efforts of advocacy. They began to realize that public institutions were not providing what they are required to provide.

In the bishops' pastoral on war and peace, their leadership on a critical issue, their broad consultation, their combining a spirituality of social responsibility with specific reflections on urgent policy questions, all provoked considerable attention within and outside the Catholic community. Furthermore, the power of their effort has

attracted attention not only to what they have to
say about nuclear weapons but also to the entire
life of a church that could produce this document.
It may well turn out that this pastoral will be the
most important tool of evangelization in our time.
For the pastoral surely makes many people wonder
about the kind of faith and understanding of life
that could lead to such a position.

Yet we know that this pastoral will not have
any lasting, beneficial effect on church or nation if
it does not become the object of careful reflection
in each parish across the nation. The efficacy of
episcopal teaching depends on the quality of
parish education and reflection programs.

Part of what is represented by both of these
events is that, just as the church has faced a
serious decline in numbers of people who faithfully
take part in church life, the church is upping the
ante regarding what it means to be Catholic.
Rather than soften the requirements of charity
and justice, these basic demands of the gospel are
being spelled out in ever clearer terms. The power
of this development depends on how well parishes
can invite people into this power of love and
justice.

It is in service to this invitation that this book
is addressed. In easy chapters and simplified style
The Parish Help Book makes the social ministry of
the parish look attractive and more than possible.
Surprisingly, in such a slim volume, Herb Weber
covers most of the key aspects of the church's
social ministry. And he does so in a way that

should encourage people to move beyond immediate service and education to the more challenging complexity of advocacy and organization of people. For this, people may have to turn to other resources which more fully address these types of social ministry. Yet, here is a primer for basic involvement.

The test of the future of the church will be how well it can combine deeper and more personalized faith with clearer and more effective leadership for justice. There is a tendency for the two to become divided and each, thereby, to become distorted. Use of this book and readiness to reach beyond these first stages to the full demands of Christian charity and justice should help to build the kind of local parish communities that can begin to meet this test.

—Rev. Philip J. Murnion
Director, Pastoral Life

AUTHOR'S FOREWORD

A few years ago my parents celebrated their 50th wedding anniversary. As the priest son, I was to have a Mass. Brothers and sisters from all over the country would be returning to Ohio with their children and grandchildren. A banquet was being prepared for other friends and relatives to join us after the Mass. Mom and Dad were both excited.

In the midst of the preparations, however, my mother had one pressing concern. That concern is what I now most remember. She carefully arranged that someone at the banquet have on hand several Styrofoam dinner takeout containers. She wanted a family member to deliver some of the anniversary celebration meal to a couple of parishioners who could not be there. It impressed me even more to learn that these lonely people whom Mom did not want to forget were neither relatives nor among the regular circle of family friends.

Perhaps my mother's desire to share her celebration of life's blessings with those who were alone and all but forgotten is an apt metaphor for this book. The following pages contain many ideas for taking our gifts and finding ways to share them with the more needy. The intention is to provide some concrete ideas while offering hope and inspiration for those who doubt their own contributions to this ministry.

Several principles have guided this work. First, the work of social ministry is not really anything new for men and women of good will. Yet, it may be very new in the sense that the times and circumstances of the 1980s are unique.

Nothing in the tradition of the Christian faith could be older than charity or service. Jesus, himself steeped in the law and prophets, quotes from Isaiah when he announces his ministry to the poor and outcasts as one of healing and providing hope (Lk 4). Where Jesus left off in his ministry of concern for the little people of the world, his followers picked up in the Acts of the Apostles. Thus Peter and John offer neither silver nor gold, but a ministry of kindness and compassion.

The history of Christianity provides many outstanding examples of charity. In the earliest church, deacons and deaconesses were responsible for material needs of community members, such as food for widows. Throughout the centuries, religious orders of men and women have been formed to care for the sick, the homeless and the destitute. In the 19th century, Frederick Ozanam founded the St. Vincent de Paul Society, thus creating one of the best vehicles in history for laity to serve the poor.

In the great social encyclicals, such as *On the Condition of Workers* (1891), *Mother and Teacher*, (1961) and *On the Development of Peoples* (1967), as

well as the Second Vatican Council's decree
The Church in the Modern World, the church stated
officially that service and social responsibility were
paramount.

Thus the topic of social ministry is not new to
this church. It flows from a rich tradition. What
may be new, however, is the present time of
response. The last 10 years have seen two significant movements come together. Although the role
of the laity has been strong since the end of the
Vatican Council, it has only recently been maturing. Laity as leaders in the church are becoming
quite evident.

Secondly, there has been a profound
reawakening of the social conscience of the
American church. The struggling national
economy may have necessitated this, but church
leadership also stimulated its development. Furthermore, the many renewal programs available
often lead their participants into social awareness.

Putting the maturing lay leadership together
with a growing consciousness of church as social
minister makes the present especially appropriate
for this work. The possibilities for service seem
almost without limit.

At the same time, the secular world indicates
a new type of volunteerism is developing. The
woman who used to raise funds for an orphanage
is now happier working directly with abused
children. Translated to church circles, the lay
response to ministry to the needy will probably
become more direct, more person-to-person than

in the past. Sunday collections and distributions of clothing are still valuable, but those services will not be acceptable as substitutes for home visits and support groups.

Noting the old-but-new flavor of parish social ministry as a starting point for this book, another principle must be added. That is, that the work of providing service to others belongs to all members of Christ's church, not just to some. Admittedly, there are only certain persons who can become actively involved in a formal and organized way—although I expect that number to grow. But the obligation to fulfill this gospel mandate is everyone's.

Therefore, the book is written with the individual's needs in mind. Much is directed toward organized parish service teams, but lots of individual items are applicable to the man, woman, or family that wants to live out a certain prompting of the Spirit to share what the Lord has provided.

Finally, although I have professional social work training, I believe that non-professionals can do more genuine service for others than they usually believe. No attempt is made in these pages to make anyone a social worker.

At the same time, however, there is usually a right and wrong way to do almost anything. That includes our attempts to help others. In order to try to help the reader draw people into the kingdom of God through service, there are ample directives offered. Sometimes real harm is done in the name of kindness; other times, the Lord manages to salvage something positive from our fumbling attempts to do his work.

Having indicated the principles behind writing this book, there is little more to say then bon voyage on the journey you are taking. For the reader who has already been actively involved in social ministry, maybe it will serve as a traveling companion that renews your enthusiasm and dedication. To the beginner there is a special caveat. These pages may give you a sense of confidence or excitement in performing this ministry of Jesus, but this book is only a guide. It does not have all the answers. What it can do is help you enter into a work that will speak to you for itself. And if you listen to the Lord in this work, then you will come to know the truth.

1

SOMEBODY NEEDS US

Step one in becoming active in social ministry is to establish a connection with the person in pain.

ON a very sultry day in the middle of July, the radio announcer stated that, according to the "comfort indicator," 85 percent of all people in the area were at the misery level. Apparently, using a graph that calculated humidity and heat, a somewhat accurate estimate of discomfort could be obtained. I'm not sure, though, that knowing I was one of 85 percent of the population made me feel better. My clothes still clung to me; I still felt lethargic and eager to find some air conditioning.

If a similar indicator could be developed for all the other kinds of discomfort and pain that people endure, I wonder how high a percentage it would register. Are more than 85 percent of all people suffering at least sometime in their lives? And if so, what kind of pain are they in? Is it the pain that should and can be relieved? In any consideration of social ministry, it is first necessary to examine what it means for someone to suffer and what is the appropiate response of a fellow Christian to those sufferers. An honest confrontation with pain will help anyone who wants to reach out to hurting people.

The existence of suffering in a world that was created by a good God has always been a theological dilemma. The presence of such great evils as Auschwitz has led some individuals into agnosticism. More personal tragedies like the sudden death of a spouse have led others into bitter hatred of a God they still believe in.

The source of pain, the experience of pain,

and the result of pain are three totally different issues. The scriptures, as well as contemporary theology—and popular philosophy—often indicate that the results of suffering can be great and beneficial. But that is not to say that the suffering itself is good. Frequently the Old Testament prophets and Jesus himself in the garden prayed that the pain would be removed. Both the elimination and the acceptance of pain have their season. A great mistake, however, is to accept what could be changed or eliminated. For example, to advise others to accept the suffering of poverty or discrimination when such evils should be eliminated is to do a disservice.

Today people in our neighborhoods and parishes are hurting in many ways. Family conflicts, unanswerable questions about raising teenagers, self-destruction through alcohol or domestic violence, and lack of work, food, or shelter are prevalent themes. And in recent years, it has become apparent that pain is not restricted to any single economic level or social class.

Pain is at its worst when it seems useless. The real tragedy of pain is not that individuals have to suffer, but that it tends to isolate persons. "Misery loves company" perhaps because a person in pain is usually alone. He or she can make others miserable, too, but still remain alone. Pain can draw people away from all those beautiful things that are associated with community. And if the common call is to establish a cohesive and unified human family, then those who in their hurting situation are withdrawn have to be the focus of our ministry.

Step one, therefore, in becoming active in social ministry is to establish a connection with the person in pain. Using this relationship as a bridge, the minister may cross over in order to help carry someone else's burden, support that person in carrying it, or work together to find ways to unload it. And there should be a constant reading of God's hand in these human cir-cumstances. Social ministry, then, means so much more than doing good things. It means entering someone else's life.

BEING SENSITIVE TO PAIN

To work with people in pain demands a sensitizing process for the minister, which begins when the person with a desire to help admits his or her own pain. We all suffer. Although the pain is much more acute for some than for others, the general characteristics are universal. I recall a brief time of pain when I dislocated my shoulder. The hurt was intense, but when the doctor in the emergency room was able to get the bone back in place, the relief was heavenly. Before he had done this, however, I felt an intense aloneness. This was the case despite the fact that two priest friends were with me. Finally, a nurse came up to me and took my hand. Only with the physical touch did I begin to realize that I could endure the pain.

Most of our pain, however, is not physical. A serious disagreement with a close friend, the feeling of abandonment by a colleague, and the aloneness in a large, strange city all hurt. We must also become aware that pain is universal and often senseless.

In the self-sensitizing processs it is good to hang onto these hurts for a moment. What if the feeling of being isolated, homeless, or without friends lasted for months instead of hours? What if our resources—loving family members, friends, prayer—had not been there? What if the physical pain, the hurt of broken relationships, and the struggle of self-doubt all happened at once? Indeed, many people suffer like this. Yet in moments of self-righteousness others are tempted to say that these people ought to learn to take care of themselves!

The preceding paragraphs are not meant to overwhelm the readers with the heaviness of world suffering. Instead, they are meant as a simple reminder that pain is very real—not foreign to us. If those in social ministry can reflect on their hurts, then they can treat others with compassion in the true sense of that word—that is, suffering with someone else. Bishop Ottenweller of Steubenville, who himself was one of the pioneers of the ministry to Ohio's migrant workers in the 1950s, indicated that the most common mistake for the volunteer visitors was to go to the camps and tell the workers how to do things better, to shape up, and become like Ohioans! That would improve their lot! The sincerity of the visitors who took time to visit strangers cannot be doubted, but the willingness to accept the others' customs and culture and try to understand their family concerns were skills that only slowly emerged.

A MINISTRY OF HOPE

When God allows us to minister to someone in pain, we become a sign of hope. Social ministry is a ministry of trust in the future of a world near despair. Jesus was able to tell Jairus "fear is useless; what is needed is trust" (Lk 8:50, NAB) as he touched the life of Jairus' daughter. So too the minister who in the name of Jesus touches the lives of others, helps them replace fear with confidence in the kingdom to come.

In this type of ministry, hope is a reminder that God cares and has not abandoned any member of his created world. The person or persons who attempt this ministry are conduits through which God's life-giving forces are pumped. Those on the verge of despair can be renewed.

One parish minister gave the example of visiting a woman who had cut herself off from God and neighbors for 10 years. Her husband had died suddenly, and she was unforgiving and angry. Much like cancer, her bitterness began to eat away at her.

A young man in her parish entered the picture when a neighbor indicated that she feared the woman's health was failing rapidly. He attempted to call on the woman, only to be told that she didn't need anyone. He was not allowed to enter the house. However, before leaving he asked the woman if it might be all right to return. She agreed to see him if he really wanted to come back.

On his return trip, the sick woman allowed the man to enter. At that time she told the story of her anger with God and how she had chosen to get even with the Lord by tuning God out of her life. She had also become lonely, easily frightened, and very accusing of "those busybodies" all around. The man listened and said very little. He visited several more times and the woman's health continued to deteriorate to the point where she had to be hospitalized. Then one day she indicated that she no longer hated God. In fact, she had forgiven the Lord for taking her fine husband and was looking forward to a chance to join him. She asked God to forgive her. The woman died a day later. It was Holy Week, and once again new life had begun.

The young man had been hesitant about his ministry at the first encounter with the woman. His gift to her, however, was to be completely accepting and non-judgmental as he listened to her. He had helped her overcome her loneliness and in the process find hope and peace.

IF NOT US, THEN WHO?

Pain is real, compassion is possible, and social ministry is filled with hope. Yet who is going to do this fine work? The modest proposal behind the following chapters is that everyone has a responsibility to share in this ministry in some way. Furthermore, everyone has both the opportunities and the talents to enter into this work.

Social ministry is not new to the Catholic Church. The St. Vincent de Paul Society is 150 years old. The Catholic Charities movement in the United States goes back to the early 1900s. Hospitals, orphanages, and homes for aging have been around for a long time. The church need not apologize unless it is to say that it has removed some of the ministry from the parish level and placed it at the level of the charities offices. Thus many parishes felt like all was being taken care of by others.

What this book speaks of, then, is a movement of concern back to parishes. Organized groups and professional social workers need not fear that they will be deprived of their work; there is plenty to go around. Rather, as the notion of personal social responsibility emerges more and more, so too does the cry of the poor, which gets louder and louder.

Not all neighborhoods have people in need of food or shelter. (Even that is more common than one would admit.) But every community has its share of disenfranchised, lonely, handicapped, or emotionally troubled. This book speaks of ministry where it is needed, beginning right around us. The reader, then, also needs to trust that this is the work of the Lord continued into the 1980s.

Finally, as the following pages unfold in specifics of social ministry, it may be possible that those who desire to minister to others may find their own pains touched and healed. After all, it is a healing ministry for both the giver and the receiver.

2
GETTING STARTED

What do I have to give? Who is hurting in this community? What can I do?

THERE is no question about finding people of good will in all parishes. The human heart can be easily stirred; ideals of compassion and genuine caring can be called to mind. A search of the sacred scriptures, a rousing homily, or the contagious atmosphere of a good workshop on social ministry can easily excite us about doing service.

But then what? Unfortunately, we have all experienced a degree of disillusion following enthusiasm simply because we did not know what steps to take next. This chapter on getting started tries to provide a vehicle for translating the reader's motivation into concrete starting points.

KNOWING SELF

At an extended training program I was conducting, I read a passage from Matthew to the audience (Mt 25:31-46). I did it as dramatically as possible and could see by smiles and nods that the commitment level of service was present. Then I asked if there was anyone who disagreed that feeding the hungry, clothing the naked, or visiting the sick would be ministry to Jesus himself. No one spoke up. I asked if they felt certain that love in action was a gospel mandate. They all agreed that it was. Was this new to them? No. Then why, I asked, did they give up 12 to 15 hours over a six-week period to listen to me talk about what they already knew? Why did they have to take a course on charity if they were already committed to it?

The almost unanimous answer came quickly.
Most of the men and women in the room felt they
needed some help. Even though they had plenty
of commitment, they were aware of barriers such
as fear—fear of failure, fear of being hurt, and fear
of being used.

Such fears can prevent some of our most inspired drives from being realized. What I admired
most in this group, however, was that they had
enough self-knowledge to perceive their fear, and
sufficient courage to admit it. That was necessary
for the fear, or any other barrier, to be overcome.

It is not wasted time for anyone contemplating
a more involved ministry to the needy to step
back and examine what he or she has to give. If
that person is a part of a group, however, then the
question is more complicated. Now the gifts of the
individuals within the group, as well as the group
as a whole, must be made clear. And even more
important, the way the group views itself is of
utmost importance. Too many attempts at service
fail because this self-perception remains fuzzy.

One parish advertised that there was going to
be a Helping Hands committee formed for anyone
who would like to work with the unemployed,
aged, or sick. Thirty men and women showed up.
They talked about what might be done. At the
next meeting nearly 20 came, and they continued
to look at issues. Eventually the group dwindled to
10 or fewer. Those who continued wondered if
they were on the Titanic and had missed the life-
boats.

The group was not willing to cast aspersions on the ones who had failed to return. Instead they tried to examine their initial announcements, the content of the meetings, and their projected goals. Only then did they discover an underlying source of confusion. To some the group was meant to be a service *planning* body for the parish and community; for most of the others, the group was simply to be a vehicle for *doing* service. As the sessions evolved into planning time, the doers absented themselves. This is not to say that doers should not be involved in planning, but the functions are distinct for the long-term purposes of the groups. Both roles are needed. Sometimes social concerns committees of parish councils are primarily planners and evaluators, while other teams of ministers within the parish are the doers. The overlap may be that the planning committees facilitate the formation and ongoing existence of the doers.

Another part of self-assessment is what already exists and can be used for further development. One group of six or eight women were already close friends. They met regularly after weekday Mass for coffee in a little restaurant down the street from the church. Each realized that they already had created a support system for themselves. If they were to embark on some collective social ministry, they would have their common prayer and affirming relationships for support.

Another similar example was a family with

five teen-age children who worked together in adopting an aged couple. Keeping up the yard, visiting and doing shopping could be more easily accomplished when it was shared by the whole family.

Most individuals have something to give whether they believe it or not. A woman who thinks that she is good only at cooking can either volunteer to cook at a soup kitchen, or offer to help teach someone with a low income or poor homemaking skills how to create tasty and nutritious meals for less money. Others, however, may not be able to cook, but are good listeners or organizers. Some are leaders. I knew a woman who professed that her gift was in scrounging. She could come up with furniture, appliances, or clothing almost upon request. Personally, I am not good at begging for items, but I know how to ask carpenters, painters, and electricians to share their skills.

Of course, faith is also a gift. Sometimes the assessment of what can be shared comes down to prayer with and for others. And if two or more persons are working together in this ministry, they simply must stop and pray at times or the whole project will dwindle to nothing. At least, nothing significant.

KNOWING THE COMMUNITY

In addition to knowing what individuals have to offer, in service to others, it is necessary to know what the community needs, what is already being offered by others, and what will be accepted. Many pastors and religious educators who have moved from one parish to another have experienced the disappointment of trying to re-create in the new setting what was very successful in the previous place, only to have it flop. Community members are different, sometimes even within short distances. Community needs can vary, and the degree of appreciation of a certain type of help can change.

Therefore, the question that must be asked is "Who is hurting in this community?" Furthermore, asking the right people this question can create a network of cooperation and can interest others who may wish to help.

One group of volunteers accepted my challenge to ask the question of who was hurting. I heard about it later when a community leader indicated to me his puzzlement that so many different people had come to him in a short period of time expressing interest in the problems of the neighborhood. They had approached the pastor, police, school principals, the welfare office, and physicians. The volunteer group was delighted in that most of the answers could be correlated. Likewise, the group felt any service it would try to develop was bound to be on target and not just based on a hunch or on one person's personal agenda.

Equally important, however, is knowing what others are already doing. Several leaders in one central city parish felt a real need for a soup kitchen because they were becoming aware of a growing number of street people. Upon investigation, however, they discovered that another church of a different denomination in the same vicinity was making plans to expand its kitchen services. Rather than create a competitive program, the men gladly joined the other group.

Even within a parish, there is often a lack of awareness of what is being done. Of course, social ministry should not be restricted to just one group; no one has the corner on the market in any area of ministry. On the other hand, there should be no sense of competition or duplication. A later chapter on the totality of parish consciousness will reflect some of these concerns.

The assessment of community needs does not have to be done in a scientific data-gathering process. Those who are dealing with community members daily can offer recommendations of what people's hurts and concerns are. A conversation with the pastor can also indicate what is being done already. Many are surprised to learn how much is happening even within their own churches.

Another more personal element can be added to the assessment procedure. I like to become acquainted with a neighborhood by walking through it. Maybe the word "walking" should be used metaphorically since many do not wish to walk on streets they do not know. Driving or riding a bicycle through that neighborhood allows me to see things on those unfamiliar streets. Sometimes I am ashamed to realize that there are little pockets of poverty practically across the block—or tracks—from comfortable homes. This very subjective experience can become more valuable than lots of data or many answers from others. In fact, this exercise can often maintain motivation for service.

Communities also have strengths. Maybe there are natural helping systems already in place, and these can be the basis for expanded services. Such helping networks may exist in ethnic neighborhoods or rural areas. Perhaps there will be extended families where relatives are close by to help each other, or next-door neighbors who will automatically assume responsibility in case of trouble. When I was growing up in a small town, the word "neighbor" was frequently used as a verb. To neighbor meant more than happening to live down the road from someone. It meant giving a helping hand, visiting, socializing, and mourning each other's losses.

Even ethnic neighborhoods and small towns have hurting people, however. And sometimes the hurts are sharper if someone feels unaccepted in a close-knit community. A very sad example of such alienation was a young woman who moved into the rural neighborhood where her husband had been reared. She bore his name and child, but remained an outsider. Her situation was complicated by severe postnatal depression, and there seemed to be no one around with whom she could talk.

One day when the husband returned from work, he heard the baby crying and then found his wife dead on the bed, the result of suicide. The town mourned, and only then became conscious of how alone the young woman must have felt.

Assessment of self, the group, the parish, or the needs of the community is not just a preliminary to doing something. It is ministry in itself as long as it is not just an academic exercise. Part of the mystery of service that women like Mother Teresa of Calcutta, Catherine de Hueck Doherty, or Dorothy Day have discovered is that an identity with those in need in itself supplies hope. It also disarms the barriers the minister may face in pursuing this work.

DOING SOMETHING

Once the person committed to service has re-viewed personal talents, group strengths, and community concerns, the simple step left is to do something. Yet, even the actions that follow can be performed in a host of ways.

Some people work best alone; they simply do not want to become members of organized helping groups. Yet they can still put charity into action by visiting someone, sponsoring a needy family, or writing to a prisoner. A woman by the name of Sharon works alone collecting clothing left from garage sales and flea markets. After making necessary repairs, she calls her local Catholic

social services office to ask for the description of a
family in need. Sharon never sees the families she
helps, but works through a caseworker. Apparently others who know her track record are only too
willing to provide clothing for use as she needs it.

Another woman watches her small-town paper
closely and whenever someone she knows is in the
hospital, she visits the person or sends a card. The
art of visiting, however, is not always easily
mastered. In a later chapter we will discuss the
skills involved.

Sometimes it is easy to fall into the Lone
Ranger syndrome. This means that someone
sincerely wants to right the wrongs of the world
and is willing to tackle that impossible job alone.
It is true that one person can make a difference,
but those tempted to work alone should remember
that even the Lone Ranger had Tonto for support
and assistance. Ministry of service often works
best when several persons are working together.

Many parishes have already organized service
teams, started conferences of the Society of St.
Vincent de Paul, or have social concerns committees. There are virtually thousands of ideas for activities that can be done by a group. However, the
service plans should respond to the concerns that
have been surfaced by the neighborhood assessment, as well as the walk through the community.

Some advantages of a group effort are that
tasks too big or frightening for one person can be
attempted, a prayerful support system can be

developed and chances for continued service are improved.

An example of an exciting group activity occurred when a team of volunteers organized to provide needed respite for parents of profoundly retarded and severely disabled children. They realized that many such parents were tied to their homes because of the condition of their children. Often couples were not able to go anywhere together—not even funerals—because one parent had to stay with a child. The group assisted by providing short-term service for staying with the handicapped child, and giving the parents a chance to get out.

Jesus worked with groups as well as alone. His debriefing of the 70 (Lk 10:17-20) is not different from the sharing that often goes on in groups after missions of service. Jesus also worked as an enabler or catalyst, another role that needs to be defined.

Functioning as an individual and working as a group are two ways to be responsive in any community. The role of catalyst is equally important. Sometimes by creating a situation in which others become socially involved is more constructive than doing the ministry itself. These catalysts are often persons with unique skills that can be used to excite others to action, help discover opportunities for service, provide the necessary know-how, and give affirming support.

A small group of young adults organized a

group called Bakers' Yeast. It saw itself as a leaven in the community. Its goals were to discover existing needs and somehow see that those needs were met. Its members encouraged able-bodied older adults to minister to the homebound aged, helped children organize a clean-up project for some of the parks they used, and worked within their own families to create a consciousness of stewardship of food.

This function of catalyst excites me. Maybe it is the teacher in me coming through. After all, many teachers are the best catalysts. Doing some private ministry alone is being true to the gospel. Working in an organized group can magnify that work. Enabling other individuals and groups to do such ministry in their own circles, however, is a privilege that transcends most of our expectations of social ministry.

The work of getting started in parish social ministry, then, includes self-knowledge, an understanding of the hurts and concerns of the community, and a plan of response. Even this strategic plan may leave some wondering what kind of specific service can be initiated. The next chapter, "Love in Action," builds on what has just been said and offers some concrete possibilities.

3
LOVE IN ACTION

Here's a smorgasbord of ideas.
Bon appetit!

CONCRETE projects or programs that relate
to contemporary hurts and needs take a great deal
of creative planning. The most benefical response
to a community problem may be simple but
previously unthought of or unneeded. If necessity
is the mother of invention, then times of greater
awareness of human needs demand inventive
thinking.

Creativity is a gift many feel they do not have.
Even those who are not creative, however, can
borrow ideas or adapt what someone else has done
under similar circumstances. This chapter is meant
for the person or group that wants to look at what
others have done. It's a smorgasbord of ideas. *Bon
appetit!*

A couple of words of caution, however, are
necessary. Because someone else's plan worked
before does not guarantee that it will be equally
successful in a different parish. Appropriate adap-
tation will be needed. The knowledge of self and
community discussed previously must still dictate
the direction of a response to human needs.

Finally, no project or program will ever replace
the personal giving of self that is behind all service. One-to-one ministry, listening to others, and
the shaping of hope and faith are always vitally
important. Those skills will be discussed in the
next chapter. For now, however, the following
ideas present a framework in which the personal
ministry can take place.

LIFE'S BASIC NEEDS

In his encyclical *Peace on Earth* Pope John XXIII clearly states that all humans are entitled to the basics needed to sustain life. Both the Old and New Testaments, as well as most of church history, reflect the same conviction. No one should be deprived of that which is needed to live.

One of the most basic of all human needs is food. Most families can do without new clothing for a while, and items like daily newspapers can be canceled. However, no one can go without food. On the other hand, for many it is the one flexible budget item. When rent or mortgage payments cannot be negotiated and the fixed income remains too low, then it is not surprising that there is less money to buy food. More than once I've been told that older people have been seen buying dog food at the supermarket. Yet these shoppers were not pet owners. Apparently the dog food was an attempt to cut their own food costs.

Any kind of sharing of food, then, seems to be paramount in providing for the needy. It is sometimes said that the real miracle of the multiplication of loaves and fishes for the crowd of 4000 was that Jesus enabled the people to start sharing among themselves the food that they already had with them. To inspire people to distribute their own food among those who are hungry is a miracle that needs to be performed more often!

Several ways of sharing food are common.

Soup kitchens, normally associated with the Great Depression or with hardcore inner-city life, have started to pop up in many areas. Often they are not held daily, but at least once a week to make sure that some nutritious food is available. It is necessary, however, to design the soup kitchen for the particular clientele. Unattached street people may be attracted to one type of setting, but families or older people will not feel comfortable mixing with them. A nutrition site for older adults should definitely be open during daylight hours, and maybe transportation will be necessary.

When the goal is not to provide daily food, but to provide improved nutrition, then maybe shopping together or a kitchen session for a small group will be necessary. Some do not know how to shop or cook. Others may know how, but have little motivation to be concerned about balanced nutrition when they are cooking for themselves.

Although going to soup kitchens or nutrition centers can literally save lives, many families simply need more food in their own homes. Often a parish food pantry can be a source of help for a family in crisis. Pantries are normally supplied by contributions on special Sundays. Running a pantry, however, requires an organizer and someone willing to be on duty at certain hours.

Recently a gleaning concept has also emerged. Moses ruled that stray grains or fallen grapes be left for the poor to glean after the harvesters had finished (Lv 19:10). This project tries to glean what food producers cannot sell. Often large companies will have boxes of cereal or other staples that are slightly below the advertised weight. The gleaners channel such food items to the poor, perhaps through pantries or soup kitchens.

Gardening has also been a way for many families to cut food costs. On a grander scale, community gardening with plots provided by the parish for those who have no room at home or for those who cannot get out is on the rise. One year I organized the parish youth group to plant a large garden for the purpose of providing fresh produce to supplement the local food pantry. (We were aware that the pantry could not take perishables, but hoped to offer their clientele the option of coming to us as well.)

The high school students became very en-thusiastic and soon the entire garden was planted. The beans, peas, sweet corn, and various types of squash started growing. I realized what a job it would be to weed the garden and harvest the crops, but it was exciting. The farming background of my ancestors was coming through. Unfortunately, in June of that year—before a single crop had reached harvest—I was transferred to another assignment. Somehow it didn't seem quite appropriate to tell the bishop that I wanted to stay in order to pick green beans. My successor agreed to work with the youth until harvest time, but the project was not repeated.

The gospels often speak about the way in which Jesus freed those who came to him from guilt, unnecessary burdens or afflictions. He enabled them to take control of their own lives, another basic human right. I especially like food cooperatives because they help people to help themselves and to take charge of one aspect of their lives.

One city parish was able to make contacts with some local farmers. Every other Saturday, farmers trucked in the fresh produce, the potatoes, and eggs. Sometimes additional items were included. Parishioners organized their own marketplace to sell the items.

The food was high quality and there was no middleman. One person remarked that even though the savings did not reduce his food bills greatly, the co-op gave him the feeling that he was no longer a victim of someone else's enterprise. Other food wholesalers were contacted as they expanded the market.

In addition to food, a chief necessity of life is shelter. This can include concern for emergency housing, longer-term dwelling places, and upkeep of homes. There are big differences between providing for the bag lady who sleeps in abandoned buildings downtown and for the family whose only heat is from the clothes dryer. Yet both are questions of shelter. Here are a few examples of creating or maintaining homes.

Sometimes a place of residence already exists, but is inadequate. For example, there may be the threat of no heat. What is needed is a friendly ad-

vocate who can advise the resident to contact the
utility companies early enough to make some pay-
ment arrangements so that services will not be
discontinued. Sometimes energy assistance programs already exist, but the person living in that
house may not know how to apply for help.

Other times the housing is simply in disrepair
and an older couple or disabled person cannot
paint it, fix the floorboards of the porch, or
replace a broken window. A couple of years ago,
under the direction of a couple of priests, a group
of high school students got together for a week in
the summer to do such repair work within their
own hometown. Prior to this, it was not uncom-
mon for teen-agers to go to Appalachia or some
large urban area to do such summer ministry. The
purpose of this new effort was to help enlighten
the kids that needy people were living right under
their noses, and there was something that they
could do about it. Some of the kids were shocked
by what they saw. But with reflection time and
communal prayer, they were able to attain a
realistic view of service. Many members of the initial group requested to do such work again. The
program has been continuing ever since.

As indicated in the previous chapter about
self-knowledge, a parish may have some skilled
persons who are willing to contribute their services
to those in need. One St. Vincent de Paul conference that I know does not hesitate to contact
plumbers, carpenters, or electricians within the
parish to ask their assistance in improving someone's home.

Providing longer-term housing may be a more illusive goal. Subsidized apartment buildings do exist, but sometimes not in sufficient number. A parish recently decided to co-sponsor the building of such an apartment complex, and worked with housing specialists to get government loans. That bold step would probably not be taken by most people beginning social ministry. Yet it is a possibility for some.

Finally, a beautiful little program that has worked was created by several churches together. With the help of some seed money, they began an interest-free loan service. Loans up to $200 were available to help pay mortgages, make small home repairs, or provide a security deposit. The loans were clearly meant to help a family get through a bad time, and therefore were normally made on a one-time-only basis. Often the money was just what was needed to help someone maintain a residence or achieve some stability. The percentage of payback on the loans was not 100 percent, so new monies were needed annually. However, there was enough payback to continue to make money available for someone else to use.

Food and shelter are primary material needs. Clothing will only be mentioned briefly because it seems to have neither the urgency nor the crisis character of the two previous issues. Thrift shops, Thanksgiving clothing collections, and rummage sales already exist. One idea that could be added, however, is to use skills to sew or remake clothing. There is no question but that there is an art connected with sewing. Perhaps creating a situation in which these skills can be shared is one of the finest ways of clothing the naked.

UNEMPLOYMENT

Recently someone said sarcastically that if a parish—or an agency—cannot provide jobs, then anything else they do for the unemployed is insignificant. I strongly disagree. Not having a job is only one of the plethora of problems connected with unemployment. Added to the need for work is learning to live within a tighter budget, coping with idle time, experiencing feelings of powerlessness, and escalating family or marital stress.

Initial unemployment may not cause great hardships. When it becomes more extended, however, and benefits are depleted, then the strain may be matched by more serious realizations. A healthy family head, for example, who has worked all his or her adult life, may be facing the possibility of applying for food stamps. This new experience also may have connotations of failure. A single parent may find that being out of work adds to tension with the children and leads to less and less patience with their antics.

These basics of life must be considered by those wishing to work in a special ministry with the unemployed. A couple of other possibilities for service at a parish level can also be added.

One group of volunteers decided to start a job hot line in their parish. Two men volunteered their home phone numbers, one for the day and one for evenings. People who had jobs to be done around the house for which a wage could be paid could contact these numbers. Available jobs were listed in the bulletin. Those willing to accept these chores could call and apply, and the small group matched jobs and workers.

Soon the hot line expanded to seasonal jobs, like nursery work in the spring. Then some employers started to use the hot line for full-time jobs. In a sense, the hot line became another type of parish cooperative. Job opportunities were posted in the parish bulletin, and the parishioners helped each other remain employed.

A more comprehensive venture was begun with the cooperation of three neighboring churches of different denominations. All three felt a need to respond to the level of unemployment they were aware of. As in many cases, they asked a church social agency to guide them in what they were to develop. But it was to become their program and their success.

One of the three churches had a room that could be used during the day as a drop-in unemployment center. Unemployed people started coming and then were asked to run the facility and keep it open. Bartering was done among the unemployed. Anyone who had something to give or request would stop in. This not only included tangible items but skills and talents. Someone ar-

ranged for a course on ways to look for hidden
jobs; that is, the ones that are not advertised.
When someone would happen to land a job or be
called back, the others would cheer.

The unemployment center also became a referral and resource center. Those who were looking
for help in counseling were directed toward family
service agencies that could provide quality services
at low cost. Lists of resources were made available
and enlivened by those who were willing to tell of
their experiences in using those resources.
Moreover, the men and women who came to the
center found it a source of support. They knew
they were not alone in facing the turbulent experience of being unemployed.

LIFE'S LOSSES

Everyone suffers major losses in life. The death of
someone close, marriage ending in divorce, and a
friendship dissolving in misunderstanding are common examples. At such times, most individuals
and families are especially vulnerable and in need
of some warmth and care. Therefore, the area of
personal loss should be included among the possible areas of service.

In addition to personal visits to those in pain,
social ministers can provide settings in which work
with the grieving can be done. A number of
parishes have established support groups for the
widowed and for the divorced.

Frequently, for example, a widowed person who has already grieved can reassure a new widow that healing is possible.

A support group is not intended to be amateur psychotherapy. I think that many conjure up the image of the hilarious therapy group on the old Bob Newhart television show and shy away from any group. Instead, these groups of widowed or divorced persons simply provide opportunities for wounded individuals to *listen* to and minister to other wounded persons, with the hope of common healing taking place.

Of course, some do not wish to be members of any group. More frequently among the widowed, there are those who are unable to get out very often. One parish chose to create a prayer network among all those who had been widowed and were aging. They were to pray for one another, and for one another's spouses. A special annual liturgy was celebrated with them. Whenever any parishioner died, they were called to pray for that person. For some of them, who feared the proximity of death, there was consolation in knowing that they, in turn, would not be forgotten by the others. Thus prayer and preparation for one's own death were being combined.

In many parishes there are those who attend all funerals so that no one will be buried from an empty church. This form of burying the dead cannot be overlooked as a truly Christlike ministry. It is a special reminder of the individual dignity of everyone, no matter how unknown he or she was in life.

THOSE WITH SPECIAL NEEDS

In every neighborhood, on every street or road, there are those who have special needs. And the persons who have special needs also have the normal needs—food, shelter, friendship—that all others have. Here two groups of persons with special needs will be included: the older adult and the handicapped.

Over 90 percent of all senior citizens in the United States do not live in nursing homes, yet the term elderly still reminds most of us of taking elementary school children to visit and sing songs at the home nearby. Not that this is bad, it is just not enough.

Older adults sometimes need and want most to be considered. Aging people can minister to others as well as anyone else. Being old is not a disease. Yet some circumstances like fixed incomes, poor nutrition, or lack of transportation do create special concerns.

Millie is a senior citizen herself. She is thankful her health is good. After retirement she began a ministry to her peers by arranging for Mass at a large nursing home, and organizing a group of home visitors. And she frequently helps arrange professional services for those whose health or self-awareness is deteriorating.

Others with less time arrange to "adopt" one older person and keep in touch, by visit or phone, on a weekly basis. The recruitment and organizing of the adopt-a-grandparent program grew out of a church Lenten project.

Frequently places of business will provide a special discount for senior citizens. One group of volunteers spent hours researching those that had such policies and published their names in a directory for the people in the neighborhood.

The federal government has a foster grandparent program that allows seniors to work with small children, giving them one-on-one attention. In this instance, the older adults are the givers instead of the recipients of service. A similar type of program could possibly be implemented in many parishes that have an elementary school. Even a couple of hours a week would allow the aging to give of themselves in what would be a valuable learning experience for the small children.

The disabled, like older adults, have special needs. They do not want to be considered incapable of doing for others. The greatest ministry with the handicapped is that which allows them to belong to the church committees. Belonging means participating and ministering.

Shirley, in a wheelchair all her life, reminded me that those times when she has been asked to minister, it has often been to pray for a retreat or renewal program at home. She asked if this was just a polite way of excluding her from the church.

To create a belonging, then, demands that the handicapped person be allowed to enter church buildings. To even get to the gathering place of the church community, transportation may be necessary. For the deaf, interpreters may be needed. For the mentally retarded, inclusion in both concrete and symbolic ways is appropriate.

As I began my work with the handicapped I discovered that most of what is being done at a parish level has been initiated by families of the handicapped. For all too many of the other parishioners, there is neither intentional avoidance nor malice, but lots of mistaken notions or unawareness. Perhaps, then, the first ministry an individual or group can do is to start waking people up. Use every vehicle possible in the parish—liturgy committees, education programs, family life ministry—to start reminding others that the handicapped not only exist in significant numbers, but are real members of that church.

I am reminded of a sign I once saw in a famous smorgasbord restaurant: "Take what you want, but eat what you take." Hopefully, the reader will do the same. As you digest what has gone before, make it your own and develop it. And know that the list of possible types of service is not complete, but so to speak, only an appetizer.

4

THE HELPING PROCESS

A person-oriented ministry involves creating a relationship, developing it through listening, and maintaining it by personal touch.

AN outstretched hand is sometimes used as a symbol of helping. The hand could be giving or receiving, but certainly it is reaching out. This symbol represents connectedness between individuals and a relationship that can become the basis of helping someone else.

The helping process, above all, demands openness. The helper has to be open to someone else's life and values. He or she has to be able to receive and listen as well as give and speak. Helping means dying to self so another can live. Unfortunately for the minister, these qualities do not usually come easily. Helping is a process that must be learned and practiced, yet it is at the center of all ministry of service.

Whether talking to a shut-in on the phone, running a food pantry, or visiting an impoverished family, the parishioner is employing the basic skills of helping. Those skills include establishing a helping relationship, listening, and visiting.

Nobody can get through life without touching others' lives in some way. It would be great if all touches were touches of healing, and all actions toward others were demonstrations of communal love. Of course, that will not likely be the case. Even the desire for a healing touch will not be sufficient in itself. There are many who bear scars from the well-intended, but nevertheless painful, words or actions of others. Rather than add to someone else's sufferings it is worthwhile learning the skills to alleviate them.

THE HELPING RELATIONSHIP

It has become commonplace to hear that someone would not accept help because of his or her pride. This is said as if to indicate a person's weakness. But there is a fine line between pride and self-respect. If self-respect is destroyed, has a person really been helped?

Whenever it becomes necessary to rely on another, a unique type of relationship is created. Whereas most relationships are based on mutuality, the helping relationship is established when an individual or family has become dependent or is on the verge of helplessness. The helper and the recipient, therefore, enter the relationship in completely different roles. This is not to say, however, that the recipient is inferior, a less worthwhile person, or lacking in dignity.

During the frequent surplus cheese distributions of recent years, men and women often expressed how surprised they were to be qualified recipients. Others indicated that they were glad that many others were able to receive as well. Both responses are indicative of the internal struggle of admitting a need but not wanting to be classified as needy. Human dignity is sometimes very fragile.

In helping people then, remember several key principles. First, allow them to maintain their dignity. Secondly, recognize that all have some right to determine their choices. Finally, avoid being judgmental of the behavior and values of others. All are hard principles to follow.

Dignity can be maintained if the helper adds a healthy dose of empathy and respect to his or her efforts. Dignity is lost when the person in need is no longer treated as being quite the special person God created. A friend who drives several residents of a nursing home to church on Sundays was appalled by a discovery she made one week. She arrived when the men were still being readied for their outing and saw that the home had only one comb that was used for the hair of all the men. Even more disturbing was a recent example of an aide using the same toothbrush for all the residents in a home for profoundly retarded adults! Any time that persons are not being treated as unique individuals, then dignity is being lost. That applies regardless of age or intelligence.

Self-determination is sometimes much harder to allow. The helper can so easily feel that he or she knows exactly what is best for someone else. Several winters ago I was working in an Hispanic neighborhood in Chicago. I met a man who was disabled but still trying to provide for a large family. His landlord refused to turn on his heat for more than a couple of hours a day. One day the man told me that the light jacket that he wore in the apartment was the only coat he had to wear outside.

I suggested that he go with me to the thrift shop on the next block to get a heavier coat. The man refused and gave what I considered a poor excuse. But I went to the store anyway and picked

out a coat I figured would fit him. When I
presented it to him, he thanked me. But the next
week, when I took him out in the cold to go to
the doctor, he was again wearing the light jacket
over a couple of sweaters. I never did see him wear
the coat. I guess he had told me once before that
he didn't want what I was offering, but I had not
listened. After all, my proposal was so sensible—at
least to me. Perhaps the man's refusal was one of
the few independent decisions he was still able to
make.

One way to help others maintain responsibility for their lives is to ask how they perceive the
problem and what steps they have already taken
to alleviate the pain. Simply put, what does the
person choose to do! I've noticed this step allows
the good-hearted assistant to maintain the role of
the freeing agent, while helping restore some sense
of independence to the one in need.

To avoid making judgments about the person
needing help is sometimes like walking a tightrope
across Niagara Falls. The occasions for falling are
obvious, and the dangers are great.

Usually the ministering person has very good
values. There is a tendency to protect these values
and not make any compromises. Therefore, it may
be hard to believe that accepting someone else
who has quite different values and behavior will
not lead to compromise, or even the appearance of
compromise.

Jesus himself provides us with the best lesson
in being non-judgmental. When the woman

caught in adultery was brought to him, he did not deny that the sin was grave. Nevertheless, he demonstrated an attitude of acceptance toward her. Non-judgmental behavior, then, does not mean being indifferent to the rightness or wrongness of an action. Rather it means being open to and accepting of the person involved in the action.

The many tasteless jokes about food stamp recipients or the perpetually unemployed are reminders of how easy it is to become judgmental. The social minister must not even become judgmental about those who crack such jokes. Even the self-righteous may need ministry.

LISTENING

The Madonna House in Combermere, Ontario, under the direction of Catherine de Hueck Doherty, has a philosophy of service, sacrifice, and prayer. Visitors are asked to become part of the community, and to accept work assignments. My job was to pick beans in the large farm area. That's where I learned a thing or two about listening.

A member of the community told me that no job was insignificant and all jobs were to be done with reverence and dedication. I attempted to pick the beans with a consciousness of their delicacy and life-giving power. Listening with my hands as I clipped off the beans, my senses came alive. The touch of the beans was matched by the feel of the breeze. My ears tuned in to the singing birds. And I was sure that the blue sky was only about two feet over my head. The ears became only one instrument for listening. With a sense of reverence and awe for all of the world, I felt like a young child who believes that he or she is the first person ever to discover a flower or a tree.

After a couple of days of this exercise, I found that the reverence and sense of oneness that I was finding in nature was also carrying over to people. When someone else spoke, I listened. This elementary lesson in listening was simply an awareness that each and every person was a part of God's creation. It felt good to discover them much as I had discovered the breeze and the birds.

Listening creates a bridge. It allows thoughts and feelings from one heart to span the gap into another. Listening means becoming part of someone else's life, at least for a moment. It is a uniquely human ability that provides a special healing. But listening can also be like dying.

Listening is dying because it does not allow one to be self-centered, and that self does not like to be left behind. The dying is perhaps most obvious when an older person finds it necessary to tell a story that the listener has heard many times before. Shutting off the aged person is probably not as life giving as continuing to listen. However, helping the storyteller finish the story and go on into unexplored territory is even more creative listening.

The Madonna House experience can be

repeated by anyone who wants to sensitize his or her listening skills. More advanced listening means finding ways to help others go beyond what they themselves first wanted to say. A husband and wife team from a parish was asked to come to a house to help a family. The mother asked them to sit at the table and talk a little. They asked her concern, and she said she worried because she could not provide enough food for the children. Then she went on and on, talking about the high price of food, the rotten factory where her husband—who was absent that day—worked, and how demanding the children were.

The visitors asked very few questions but indicated that they were interested in her problems. When the man said that he agreed it probably was hard to feed a family sometimes, the woman broke down in tears and cried, "Especially when your husband drinks up the paycheck at the bar." She then indicated that she was afraid to say this at first because the couple might think ill of her husband. She was scared of what would happen to the family and she really did love her husband.

That is a typical example of how compassionate listening allows someone to trust and then share a vital part of his life. Had the couple said something like "You are better off than all those people in Bangladesh who have no food," the woman most likely would have ended the conversation. Pietistic answers—people still say "offer it up"—simply block someone from getting to their real hurt. And it is hard to minister when you don't even know what the true need is. Likewise, the couple could easily have fallen into the trap of substituting material assistance for the real help of spending time and giving of self.

Sometimes listening means helping clarify the request. This is not done with Gestapo-type questions, but with the same reverence and respect that any of God's special creatures deserve. Often the request leads to an emptiness and longing. When Jesus talked to the woman at the well, she asked for his type of water so she wouldn't have to work so hard. Soon, by clarifying her concerns and by listening between the lines he helped her realize she was a very troubled person looking for hope and someone to believe in again. Listening has the power of giving such hope and faith.

VISITING PEOPLE

A friend was calling on an older Italian woman who feared leaving her house. She was glad to have a visitor and offered him a cup of coffee. On his second visit, she had the coffee already prepared and also gave him some pastries. On the third visit, he had spaghetti and dessert. The menu did not stop there. Soon there were two entrees, wine, and of course the dessert. The man admitted that he liked to eat and seldom complained.

Most visits, however, need not become social calls. In fact, one of the key points is to have a clear understanding of the purpose of the visit. A home visit could be considered an invasion of privacy, so it should be taken seriously and be thought through. Making the purpose of the visit clear to the resident prevents fear and misunderstanding. It is comforting, for example, for an older couple to know that the visitor is there to help arrange transportation to church and not to plan the couple's entrance into a nursing home.

Most visits to homes come about with some prior arrangement. If the visit is not actually the result of an invitation, it may at least have developed from a contact. For example, someone may ask for help. The parish service policy may be that a home visit will first be made to talk about the situation. Even with that arrangement, however, there should be some common courtesy and an attempt to call ahead. Trying to stop in just to catch someone else off guard indicates that the whole foundation of this ministry should be reconsidered. Social ministers are neither judges nor policemen.

Visiting people at places other than home can be extremely awkward. Again, a clarification of the purpose of the visit is helpful. Visiting a stranger who may not want to talk to anyone is hardest of all.

I recently was asked to stop by a hospital to talk to a dying man about reconciling with his son. Neither the man nor the son knew me, and the man could have thrown me out of the room. So I asked the woman who wanted me to make the visit if I could use her name to tell the man that someone was concerned. She gave me permission.

I introduced myself to the man in bed, told him who had asked me to come, and expressed a desire to talk with him. Then when he agreed to talk, I felt that I could start to develop a theme of readiness for death. In a second visit we touched on the topic of his relationship with his son. That was all that was needed. The man's wife, who had been there both times, facilitated the discussion after that. Suddenly she was enabled to minister within her own family.

Multiple visits to the same person or family can allow an authentic helping relationship to develop. Yet the clarity of purpose must be ever present. Unless the visit is to provide a social life, as with the aging Italian woman, mixing socializing with other types of helping does little but confuse the issues. Of course, that does not mean that visitors are unsociable or cold; they should be straightforward and honest.

Lastly, a visitor is often most successful when working with a partner. Fear of the unknown is lessened when one is not going alone. Opportunities for misunderstanding are minimized. Moreover, with two visitors, it is easier to catch all the nuances of the conversation in order to really listen to the one in need.

The process of helping another involves creating a relationship wherein there is preservation of dignity and self-reliance. Listening is an instrument for developing and maintaining that relationship, and the visit is a valuable opportunity for this person-oriented ministry to take place.

5

GOOD USE OF RESOURCES

At times, the helper will need the community to assist, but making referrals is an art, and community resources need to be discovered and explored before being used.

WILLIE had been living in his car for four
months when he happened to attend Mass at
rural St. Mary's. After Mass he asked a friendly
looking woman if he might have some food. She
directed him to Paul, who coordinated the social
ministry of the parish.

Paul took Willie home and gave him some
stew. Then Willie talked. He was about 20 years
old, had been in the psychiatric wards of several
hospitals, and was sure that he didn't want to go
back to the city where he had been living with an
uncle and aunt. Above all, Paul discovered, Willie
was extremely fearful—perhaps paranoid—and
suspicious of anyone who he thought might be
tampering with his mind. On the other hand,
however, he wanted some shelter besides his car.
Paul knew that he could put him up in the little
motel in town, but wasn't satisfied that that would
be enough.

Simple referral of Willie to some agency would
not work because Willie would not have gone. Yet
Paul knew his own limitations. True help for
Willie would mean something more than beef stew
and a motel room. So Paul called a professional
social worker for consultation. Since Paul felt that
in the course of the evening Willie had at least
begun to trust him, he himself must remain the
agent. With the help of some advice and coaching,
he might eventually lead Willie to the next step.
The consultation focused on what Paul as a
layman could do to help Willie retrace some of his
steps and discover for himself what he needed.

This story dramatizes a healthy use of community resources. It conveys the notion that any man, woman, or family that is ministering may need to call upon others for assistance.

Using what is already available in a community allows some networking to take place. Before resources will be used well, however, two other steps must be considered. The art of referring someone to an individual or an agency for help must be developed. People often get lost between their first contact, the person in the parish, and the professional person that they may really need to see. Secondly, the resources that exist in a community must be discovered and explored before being used. There is no sense in referring people to a place that cannot help them anyway. This chapter will treat both the manner of making referrals and the development of a resource system.

MAKING REFERRALS

Although it is not likely that Jesus was referring the lepers to the priests for help, I think that if Jesus were walking in our complex world, he would try to use all the resources at his disposal.

The appropriate time for making a referral is as important as the manner in which it is done. And the appropriate time is when it is needed and acceptable to the person in need.

Often people will come to a fellow parishioner

or to a neighbor because they feel no threat of being psychoanalyzed or that their need will be made public. Yet referring the person seeking help to an agency may mean changing from a safe to a fearful situation.

A priest recently called with a great dilemma. He was working with a family in which a father had sexually abused a child. The family was now resolved to struggle together and work out its problems. Yet they knew that if they were to go anywhere else for help, that law required that the father be reported to the Children's Protection Services. Since it was a small community, there was a belief that the family's problem would soon be made public.

The priest checked with the prosecuting attorney. He discovered that he was exempt from reporting the family. Any referral, however, would open up the case. In addition, the family protested they would not follow through with the counseling. At the same time—and the priest was keenly aware of this—not referring might mean further abuse in the home. Sometimes it simply is not easy to know whether or not to make a referral.

To help make a judgment on whether or not to refer someone, try to decide if the professional or agency can provide more than the parish volunteer, and insure that you are not making the referral just to get rid of someone. It is also very important that the referral is mutually acceptable.

Perhaps there are twin evils here. One is to try to do everything by yourself. The other is to send everybody to some other place or person. People in parishes do not have food to feed the world, but maybe they can feed a family. They cannot house a destitute couple for a year, but maybe they can shelter them overnight. They cannot visit every patient in every nursing home in the city, but they can spend time with Helen in 211. When the person in need requests what the parish social ministers have to offer, there is no need for referral. Use of other resources comes about when their needs go beyond that which one person or group can offer.

When it comes to the "how" of making referrals, I believe in letting those in need do as much as possible. Hand-holding may be necessary for someone who is feeling deeply depressed or inadequate. Some may indeed have a difficult time getting up the courage to call for help. The parish minister may have to give the phone number or even dial the phone—but let the one with the request do the talking. This approach, in fact, is ministry in itself because it allows the other person to start assuming responsibility.

Sending someone to a soup kitchen or pantry, where no appointment is needed, is quite simple. It is important to remember, though, that the volunteer doing the sending must know that the client will qualify for the help sought.

RESOURCES

If there were ever a golden calf in social ministry, it would have to be the often touted Resource Book. Committees mimeograph pages of resources, participants at workshops beg for the books, and those who have them cling to them more than Linus to his security blanket.

As a result, there are more resource listings around than most people need. The sad truth, however, is that having multiple lists of agencies who specialize in anything from respite care to home gardening does not make one a better minister or even, for that matter, better able to use these resources. In other words, having the book that is filled with information may be worse than having to research one's own places for referral.

Rather than just collecting various resource books, I would suggest writing your own. This does not mean that any book that is available in your city or county is worthless. But use it like a dictionary. Look up names and numbers. If and when they are worthwhile, transfer them to your own book.

In writing your own book, it might be wise to create categories of interest. Most people want to have some listing of where food is available. Maybe doing some questioning can help. Is there more need for food delivery in the form of a food pantry or of a soup kitchen? Is there a food co-op or Meals on Wheels? Once the issue of food is well explored, then do the same reasoning with shelter (overnight, long-term, women and children, men), and so on.

In other words, start by raising questions before looking for answers. (Perhaps use the categories from Chapter Three as a guide.) Then find the community resource book that you picked up at the last workshop. Start answering your questions. When in doubt as to its function, call the agency listed.

Once there is a need to make a referral, then the real information starts to pour in. Under the listing of the resource used, it helps to write what the result was, who is good to talk with at the agency, and what restrictions may exist.

Whenever several parishioners, who are in-volved in service, happen to sit down together, they will invariably compare notes. Someone at the gathering will start to talk about a success or failure in using a resource. Others will add insights based on their own experiences in that area of need. I have learned much about using what's available during such gatherings.

Of course, there also emerges the possibility of unofficial helpers. Those are the ones whose names will never be listed in a community resource book, yet they may know exactly how to provide assistance. I'm reminded of a particular school principal who happens to have access to shoes and coats.

By this time, the new resource book is really taking shape. It may be less complete than the one that an agency may print, but it will probably be one book that will get used.

The process of writing this book will probably surface one other concern. Areas in which there are no places—or only skimpy listings—for referral will appear. These gaps, like transportation for the handicapped or shelter for battered spouses, may indicate a priority to the ministers.

USE OF NATIONAL RESOURCES

For the most part, the presentation on resources has included ways to know and to use what's in any given community. Local resources are different from city to city or county to county, but it is where help is most likely found.

It may be valuable, however, not to stop with local listings. Nationally known centers and organizations differ from local resources in that their value is primarily found in educational or lobbying efforts. Sometimes affiliation with the national programs can help the individual at the local level keep a broad perspective. Likewise, the organizations often provide ideas of how parish communities elsewhere are dealing with similar problems.

There are hundreds of organizations and associations. Many have newsletters—although subscribing to a newsletter can sometimes provide the same false security that I associate with resource books. Many publish special pamphlets.

The following listing is minimal. Most of the titles explain the organization's purpose. A few, like the U.S. Catholic Conference or the National Conference of Catholic Charities, are many-faceted. The reader would have to inquire about materials in a specific social area or request a list of publications.

U. S. Catholic Conference
Office of Peace and Social Development
1312 Massachusetts Ave., N.W.
Washington, D. C. 20005

National Conference of Catholic Charities
1346 Connecticut Avenue, N.W.
Washington, D. C. 20036
(Publishes monthly *Charities, U.S.A.* and semiannual *Parish Outreach Review*)

Campaign for Human Development
1312 Massachusetts Ave., N. W.
Washington, D. C. 20005

NETWORK
806 Rhode Island Ave., N. E.
Washington, D. C. 20018
(Catholic social justice lobby)

Bread for the World
6411 Chillum Place, N. W.
Washington, D. C. 20012
(World and domestic hunger issues)

Food Research Action Center
1319 F Street N. W.
Washington, D. C. 20004
(Food stamp legislation and Food for Children)

National Low Income Housing Coalition
215 Eighth Street, N. E.
Washington, D. C. 20002

National Neighbors
Bowen Bldg., Suite 332
815 15th Street N. W.
Washington, D. C. 20005
(Equal Housing Opportunity Promotion)

National Committee for Full Employment
815 16th Street, N. W.
Washington, D. C. 20006

National Catholic Conference for Interracial Justice
1200 Varnum Street, N. E.
Washington, D. C. 20017
(Programming for Interracial Justice—informative
newsletter)

Nursing Home Advisory & Research Council, Inc.
Concerned Relatives of Nursing Home Patients
P.O. Box 18820
Cleveland, Ohio 44118
(Bimonthly newsletter *Insight*)

National Catholic Office for Persons with Disabilities
1200 15th Street, N. W.
Suite 102
Washington, D. C. 20005

The Healing Community
139 Walworth Avenue
White Plains, N. Y. 10606
(Newsletter for parishes ministering to handicapped)

National Catholic Rural Life Conference
4625 N. W. Beaver Drive
Des Moines, Iowa 50322

Pax Christi
6337 W. Cornelia
Chicago, Illinois 60634
(Coalition of Catholics for international peace)

6

CONTINUING STEPS

Necessary tools with formidable sounding titles such as "advocacy," "organization," and "education" can become simply other names for caring, compassion and healing.

A story is told about the famous Mayor Fiorello LaGuardia of New York City. A woman was arrested and brought before him for having stolen a loaf of bread. When he asked her to state her plea, she admitted that she had stolen the bread, but only because she was desperate to feed her children. LaGuardia indicated that the law was clear, and the woman would have to be fined for punishment. But then he added, since the city allowed such a situation to exist in which a woman would find it necessary to steal in order to feed children, a collection would be taken among the others in the room to pay the fine.

Anyone who has already been involved in some type of social ministry will immediately recognize situations much like this. Providing a meal and a place to live is important, but re-creating a society in which no one will have to go without food or shelter is even more important. This chapter looks at making attempts to re-create the community. I call it "Continuing Steps" because I see a direct connection between this and the types of ministry—helping the lonely, the sick, handicapped, older adults, or unemployed—mentioned in previous chapters.

The guidelines stated in Chapter Two about self-assessment and knowledge of problems and concerns still apply for this type of work. There is no sense in restructuring a community if that community is already healthy. Furthermore, the old idea of not throwing out the baby with the bathwater will gently remind everyone that even when these further steps are required, there is much good that should be preserved and built upon.

Several possible continuing steps are advocacy, organization, and education. Hopefully, these rather formidable terms will look as inviting as words like caring, compassion and healing ministry. Truth is, advocacy, organization, and education are simply additional tools for providing a healing touch and a compassionate service.

ADVOCACY

Not long ago someone who has been working with the unemployed by providing food or material goods called to ask me about the next step. His remarks were that their parish service team had been helping many families in need but were realizing that something greater was necessary. Assisting someone through the month with a food order was not helping that person get retrained for a new job.

Advocacy is an extremely Christlike form of service because it attempts to give power to the powerless and a voice to the voiceless. Interestingly enough, sometimes those who need power at a given time in their lives are the same ones who were normally on top of things. Many of the long-term unemployed of recent years, whose benefits had terminated, found themselves powerless for the first time. On the other hand, sometimes the ones we consider perennially powerless have power when it comes to understanding and working through a welfare system. I have a consultant who helps me understand some of the disability requirements. This woman has little voice in society because of her various handicaps. Yet she is articulate in knowing the right contact persons, how to apply, and what will be required in the areas of disability.

Being an advocate as a form of parish ministry requires courage, a spirit of adventure, and plenty of perseverance. A well-educated and assertive woman volunteered to help someone else make first application for general relief. She got up at 4:30 a.m. to get to the office in time. She waited with the other person for a couple of hours, only to be told that the quota had already been taken for that day. The next day, she got up at the same time, waited in line again, and finally was able to see a caseworker. Then the real ministry began. Some of the forms and many of the questions were so hard for the client to understand that the woman often had to translate them into simpler words and speak on the client's behalf.

Often advocates have to contend with their own anger. Finding stores, government departments, or even churches that make things impossible for the less educated, the disabled, or minorities, can create great anger among advocates who are doing this ministry of walking along beside someone in need. This anger can be channeled creatively. Allowed to run rampant, it will ultimately become destructive, forcing the advocates to simply give up or become ineffective.

Channeling anger means using it to cause change. When the advocates work with powerless people in a situation that tends to depersonalize, it is easy for them also to feel powerless. That's when the realization dawns on many that some bigger change is necessary. Change within a system, however, may take both a type of organization and education of the public.

ORGANIZATION

A group of mothers of severely and profoundly retarded children discovered that their children were not being allowed any special consideration. The state they lived in was glad to count the children for census purposes, which allowed an increase in government support, but accorded no monies or assistance— not even what was available for the less retarded—because their developmental disabilities were so severe. The parents felt that they and their children were being used. Meanwhile, planning for the future of their children, which was too big a task for them, was left totally in their hands.

Realizing that no change would take place unless they pushed for it, they organized and soon found themselves surprisingly powerful politically. No longer was it the voice of one or two persons, but the sway of three or four hundred. They did their homework, formulated clear goals, and then they pursued them relentlessly. They knew that their children had the same rights as other children, and eventually those rights were respected. It is a fine example of advocacy for a voiceless group of people that has been accomplished through organization.

Organization allows political activity. Being political means more than writing to legislators—although I have learned that that has a surprising influence. Political action means several voices becoming one and influencing those who represent the people.

A group of individuals chose a ministry to persons in a nursing home. They were happy to visit and spend time with some very lonely and neglected individuals. Soon they realized that there were some injustices in the home. The food was poorly prepared, the nursing staff was inadequate, and some of the residents told horror stories of mistreatment and abuse.

This group, which had begun as a direct-service team, found that it was becoming frustrated. Its work had been like applying bandages when surgery was necessary. After investigating and making contacts with supervisors, families of residents, and consultants, the group discovered that appropriated money for the home was being used by the owner for another business project that was failing. Eventually, the group contacted a legal assistance group that was able to take the entire case to court. In the end, the service to the individuals was much improved. Furthermore, this nursing home was no longer giving a bad name to the many other good facilities.

A common goal or purpose is necessary for organization to take place. Usually people will gather around the same special interest, like improved protection for the unborn, or insurance of the rights of older adults. People also gather because they live in a common geographical area. Neighbors may not agree on appropriate remedies but they may be willing to band together to improve their own neighborhood.

Good organization includes several necessary preliminary activities. Selecting those who are truly interested in improving the situation is paramount. Often some people wish to blow off steam but are of little support because they will not follow through on any plan. It is better to work with a small dedicated group than a large one that just wants to make a splash.

Secondly, do research well. Facts are more important than preliminary bias. In the nursing home example it would have been tempting to create a stink before knowing anything at all about the actual injustices in management. On the other hand, just because people feel mistreated does not mean that they have been victimized.

Finally, write both a statement of the problem that is being considered and the steps needed to act on it. The statement will help unify all members, a factor that is necessary for any organization. The best way for a group to lose credibility is for its different members to disagree in stating what the problems are.

Next is the process of taking the proposed steps, contacting other individuals—especially appropriate leaders who are interested in the same point of view—and occasionally caucusing to clarify the issue and map out new plans of action.

Organizing will have long-term effects but it usually is not done overnight. Stirring a community into a frenzy over an issue may create great press, but it may not make significant changes. A story is told about a group of citizens who in the early '70s had one of their first chances to express themselves on the issue of run-down housing and filthy living conditions in their city. They managed to get a hearing with County Health Department officials. According to witnesses, one of the residents carried a jar of cockroaches into the meeting. The jar was empty when they left. An expression of concern had been made; the public had been informed. Nevertheless, the great drama of releasing a hundred cockroaches in the health department offices was of little value without an organized follow-up.

More frequently the less-than-dramatic channels to be taken by a group will include meeting with board members of the facility under question or contacting the appropriate elected officials. Also, it may be important to make a viewpoint known through "letters to the editor" or publications. Finally, negotiating with landlords, heads of corporations, or those specifically responsible for an area of community life can help bring about change.

EDUCATION

The term education is used here not to represent a
formal setting of learning, like a school or univer-
sity, but a style of attempting to change a society.
Maybe all social ministry is educational; when
someone or some group in a parish is ministering
to the needy, it is educating others to the role of
social ministry in the Christian community, and
having specific healing consequences on the entire
population of an area.

A small, rural, mostly Catholic community in-
vited me to assist in long-term planning for its
social ministry. We did some self-assessment and
community assessment, and most of the community leaders in the group said that their primary
concern was the abuse of alcohol by adolescents.
Deaths of several young people in auto accidents
connected with alcohol had started to alarm
parents. Furthermore, alcohol abuse was having
other effects on the behavior of the youth at
school and home. Yet, according to the group, in-
dulging in alcohol was all but encouraged by the
parents in both their lifestyle and implicit values.

The strategy for ministry, then, had to go
beyond providing ways to help those individuals
who were suffering. (That was included, too, by
the way.) A massive community re-education process was begun, aimed at both adolescents and
their parents. The group even planned to
challenge some sacred traditions like serving beer
at all festivals and allowing unrestricted entry to

the serving areas. In addition, the re-education was to include providing speakers for any and all organizations of the community.

The result of this massive undertaking is not known yet. Without a doubt, some members of the community may have less need to do direct ministry to those hurt by abuse of alcohol. Certainly there may be more support for, and understanding of, those who do seek help.

Not all education efforts are this extensive. Couples experienced in raising children are educating when they work with younger couples on parenting. So are individual members addressing their clubs on what they have found to be social concerns. This book is even an educational effort.

Some social issues are worldwide in scope. The person at the local level cannot make changes alone, but can be of help if networked with other concerned men and women around the nation or world. Thus, nuclear arms or world hunger can easily escape a conscientious response by the local parishioner unless there is significant education.

Education on issues of global consequence demands an effective way of bringing home the topic—one that motivates positive response and not simply guilt.

Practically everyone has seen a sufficient number of pictures of starving children in Africa. Sometimes the pictures motivate the viewer to make a contribution. Real education must also help the learner develop a new respect for the use of food and a concern for food distribution. That is, education as a means of social change must be capable of leading people to live in new and healthier ways with a renewed awareness of the plight of others in the world.

Sometimes the individual hurts that all ministers encounter lead them to start thinking about taking additional steps to heal the crippled world that causes those hurts. Jesus' Sermon on the Mount seems to go beyond touching the lives of individuals by recommending values for rebuilding society. Through advocacy, organizing, and education, the work of rebuilding still goes on. It is always necessary to remember that just as an individual or a family may feel broken, deserted, or hopeless, so too can a community or a society express its own type of brokenness. Often to heal or help an individual or a portion of a community, the whole community must be addressed. Thus it, too, becomes healed, and further pain to individuals is lessened.

7

TOTAL PARISH MINISTRY

Parish social ministry is not apart from parish life,
but a part of all that the parish is and does.

A pastor recently indicated that since Vatican II, he felt that his parish had become a member of the program-of-the-month club. Every area of ministry, from children's liturgies to evangelization had its own workshops and was recommended as the parish's first priority. Parishes today have many committees and groups—support groups, prayer groups, study groups, and planning groups whose job is to coordinate all the other groups!

This isn't to say that groups and committees are bad in themselves. There are dangers, however, and one of those is that parishioners can divide themselves into areas of specialization and forget that the other areas exist. St. Paul said it eloquently in his letter to the Corinthians. The eye and the ear are equally important to the body. Both are necessary and neither can replace the other. Parishes need liturgists as well as educators and youth workers. The social ministers must respect the other aspects of parish life as they must be respected for their work.

Part of my dream, however, is that social ministry be practiced by all parishioners, even those who cannot be very active. After all, social responsibility is an integral part of the gospel, not an elective. Perhaps a parallel in the world of liturgy would be the desire to include all parishioners in the celebration of the Eucharist although only some may be called to be lectors or deacons. Social ministry is a ministry for all in the parish even when only some can be active in an organized way.

The second part of the dream is that the mentality of serving the needs of others will be incorporated into other parts of parish life. The women's group or the youth council may already have service programs. Can these be highlighted? Is it possible for the liturgy committee also to develop a social conscience or the CCD teachers to include social ministry in their curriculum?

The thesis of this chapter is that all of these questions can be answered in the affirmative. When the idea of social ministry is integrated into the fullness of parish life, then something else very special will happen. Then the particular group or team ministering to the needy will achieve a very real service to all the parishioners. They will share the privilege of serving those who are in pain.

GENERAL RULES FOR INTEGRATION

St. John's Parish has always been a leader. It is one of those rare parishes that has articulated its mission statement, has a highly sophisticated structure relating to contemporary ecclesiology, a developed lay leadership, and boasts a broad base of parishioner involvement.

A pastoral associate at St. John's called to ask for consultation. She indicated that the parish had an active St. Vincent de Paul conference, a personal family ministry team, and a group of former parish retreat leaders, who were all interested in different aspects of social ministry. The associate's concern was that these three groups not compete.

Maybe that's the kind of problem many parishes would love to have. But it can be quite a challenge. An understanding of the healing ministry of Jesus is becoming more evident to many today. Sometimes it comes about through retreat, prayer groups, or family and marriage ministry. And when there are many who find a new consciousness of this sort, then the problem is to channel their energies.

Interest groups need not compete, but they do not necessarily have to become one large group either. The three groups at St. John's met and worked out some common assessment of parish needs as well as common goals. This headed off the possibility of any conflict or animosity among them. Then they decided which group could undertake which ministry most effectively. The point was to see their work as part of the whole.

Competition can be incredibly destructive. As parishioners seek to strengthen their ministry to the needy, they will certainly find there are enough concerns to go around. First they must foster a healthy respect for others who have similar desires to serve.

A second important rule for social ministers is to avoid secrecy. Obviously not every person who visits a sick neighbor needs to talk about it. But when there is an organized parish group trying to assist others, it can do the parish a favor by making known the type of work it is doing. Observing confidentiality does not preclude making a regular report to the parish. This stewardship report might be most appropriate if parish funds or special collections are used by the group.

Not being aware of what is going on can also be avoided by calling on the whole parish to participate in such things as food and clothing collections, and urging those with special skills to help out with particular projects. Mentioning the work of the social ministers in the general intercessions of the Mass enables all to be a part of their work. Finally, talking of their work at school or CCD can help spread enthusiasm and awareness of social ministry.

Finally, a word of caution to the leaders of ministry teams: Avoid getting trapped in power struggles. Charismatic and gifted individuals, often leaders with a great deal of dedication and sincerity, can suddenly discover they are involved in building their own kingdoms, not necessarily in extending the kingdom of God.

Kingdom building can sneak in even though the person simply feels that he or she is trying to organize and direct the ministry. It is good to become aware of its symptoms. Some of its telltale signs are: others fear disagreeing with the leader or asking him or her to accommodate them; competition with other parish efforts is more common than cooperation; more effort is spent keeping the ministry program alive than in actual ministering; leaders take easy offense when the pastor, parish council, or even other team members don't seem to take the work as seriously as they do; finally, these leaders find themselves whistling "I did it my way."

Perhaps these indications of kingdom building are true for any parish committee. The attitude of running their own show, however, is especially inappropriate for social ministers who are to be leaders in compassionate understanding. Perhaps the final chapter on ministry among social ministers provides the necessary antidote for those afflicted by the kingdom-building disease.

IDEAS FOR EDUCATORS

Teachers have many opportunities to integrate social ministry into their classes. The challenge is to integrate social ministry into the whole day of school and into the very fiber of the school or catechetical structure. Setting aside one course on justice or charity is not enough. Opportunities for teaching concern for those who are hurting must be used as they occur. A course in social studies or English may have the same potential as a discussion during the religion period. Likewise, justice within a classroom and a keen eye for developing the young person's senses of empathy are ongoing goals.

One teacher was in the midst of a unit on personal letter writing. She chose that time to teach another lesson as well, namely that letter writing is a very powerful tool in reaching lonely individuals. She contacted a nearby nursing home and received the names of residents to whom the students could write.

The students labored over the initial letters, but real excitement hit the class when the older adults started to answer the letters. This gave the students a firsthand experience of the feedback from service. Ongoing correspondence was then encouraged but not forced.

The teacher soon learned that the project had a greater impact than anticipated. Out of modesty, the whole project had remained somewhat quiet between her and the principal. The students, however, went home and started talking to their families about how they had been visiting the residents of the nursing home with their letters. Soon the brothers and sisters of these students came back to school and encouraged their teachers to start similar projects.

Often a service project can be a part of the total curriculum for the year. Integration with the other activities and concerns among the students is necessary for good planning. Some helpful hints in planning follow.

Begin with the needs that have already presented themselves in the classroom. What is an area of concern for the teacher or among the students? A likely example that will be developed here is the way the boys and girls at an elementary level often make fun of someone who is different, for example, a student with a disability or one from a particular ethnic background. Discussing how it feels to be left out or laughed at is good preparation for service to others.

Another help is to talk about the unique qualities of all members of the human race, or to expose the students to unique people in history or literature. If the discussion centers on the disabled, read about Helen Keller, or discuss the life of a popular blind singer.

If racism is the concern, present information on the minorities involved. Or play a game of discrimination in the classroom by using hair and eye color as a basis of judgment and bias. The story of the Good Samaritan is a good illustration of the goodness of a member of a minority group.

Depending on the age of the students, perhaps the service project should be no more than visiting or inviting in a handicapped person in order to understand him or her better. For older students, it would be good to trade something with a disabled person. This will help show that the handicapped do not always have to be on the receiving end. Perhaps the class can arrange to plant some seeds in a flowerpot and exchange it for something the handicapped person specializes in. A friend of mine, crippled by cerebral palsy, designs pictures on a typewriter by using the characters to make the straight lines or circles she cannot construct freehand.

After completing the trade, the topic of discrimination can be brought back to the classroom to help the students examine who else is special and if there are any conclusions they can draw. The teacher should fully support the feeling of success in the project. Finally the teacher can consider ways to continue the project, like keeping contact with the minority or handicapped person.

For older students most of the recommendations for preparing for and picking a successful project, and the subsequent reflection and application to similar needs, would still apply.

With high school students I have sometimes arranged simulation exercises—for example, what it's like to be old—before doing any service project. Making the project sound like fun is not really misleading because service can be most enjoyable. Thus 60 high school students can look forward to going through a starvation day to raise money to feed the hungry if the day is appropriately planned.

In all of this, there is another valuable message the teacher is sharing. That is that individuals and groups of any age really can make a difference in the world.

SOCIAL MINISTRY AND LITURGICAL CELEBRATION

A priest told me that the last thing that he wanted was to spend all his preaching time on social problems. Although I suggest it is good to spend some of our time preaching the gospel response to social problems, this small section is meant to go beyond homily helps.

A liturgical celebration is supposed to be the coming together of the community in praise and

thanksgiving to God. In that context, the development of the faith community is fostered, and the
prayer for the ongoing growth of the kingdom
that Jesus preached is presented. As liturgist
Father Nathan Mitchell, OSB, states, liturgy must
remind the participants of the perfect world to be,
but be grounded in the less-than-perfect world we
live in. By its nature, then, liturgy cannot allow
itself to be divorced from a ministry of love to
others.

For liturgical celebration to be connected with
social ministry it must not be isolated from the
lives of the men, women, and children who gather
each Sunday. In itself, it must be a reminder of
the pains and sufferings that real people experience each week. Sometimes after celebrating
Mass in a parish, I have been approached by
people who ask if I was, by any chance, listening
in on their conversation at breakfast that morning. The homily, or even the choices of prayers or
songs, apparently offered direct hope-filled responses to their concerns. Truth is, the saltshaker
on their kitchen table was not a hidden
microphone, but listening to the concerns of many
during the week may have been precisely what
kept me in touch with the daily struggles we all
share.

Regarding the Eucharist, the saving act of
redemption that is celebrated is a promise of
liberation from pain and suffering. That is noted
specifically in the words of Eucharistic Prayer IV,
when the celebrant says, "To the poor he pro-

claimed the good news of salvation, to prisoners, freedom, and to those in sorrow, joy." Those are rather exciting words about the way in which this celebration should affect our lives.

Within that setting, then, it would be helpful for the liturgy planners to be conscious of their brothers and sisters in pain and try to offer some glimmer of hope.

A few ideas that might start the planners thinking include: Begin with the liturgical cycle of readings and feast days. Feasts of saints that are known for charity or justice can be celebrated. The Sunday readings from Luke, every third year, are special times of remembering the outsiders whom Luke recognized so well. Any other scripture reading that comes up in the normal course of readings may challenge the receptive liturgy committee to develop a theme that is truly biblical.

I remember one day telling the bishop who had asked me to study social work, that I was sure that the Bible had not changed during those two years of graduate studies. Yet suddenly there were passages that I had never before noticed about serving the poor and Jesus' love for the oppressed. I guess that the Bible hadn't changed, but I had.

In addition to the church calendar, there are some very significant national holidays that can be celebrated liturgically with a real sense of concern for others. Two days that are most common are Thanksgiving, when many parishes collect food or clothing, and Labor Day, which can be observed

with special regard for the unemployed. These, as
well as many other holidays, are times when
parishioners are extremely sensitive to what the
good news can offer them.

Other occasions offer opportunities for special
liturgies to be celebrated for particular groups. A
Mass for the retarded children in the special
education class, Eucharist with the senior group,
or a liturgical celebration with the widowed in
behalf of their deceased spouses can help everyone
connect liturgy and their life concerns. Those
especially afflicted may even by used for the
various ministries at the Mass. For me, a highlight
for several years has been the weekly celebration
of Eucharist with teen-agers in the juvenile deten-
tion center. Themes of freedom and forgiveness
have a special impact for me as well as for those
young people.

Lastly, on a frequent basis, all liturgical
celebrations can include intercessions and remem-
brances of those who are suffering. When this is
done, there is a constant reminder of the univer-
sality of Christ's love, a love that draws us to
share his concern for the needy.

Parish social ministry, therefore, is not apart
from parish life, but a part of all that the parish is
and does. Those who are in social ministry in a
direct way dare not jealously guard their
apostolate, but rejoice in the Lord when others
hear the same call. Social ministry must be shared
and celebrated liturgically with all the people of
God.

8

DON'T STOP NOW

You need a survival kit: play, pray and minister to one another. See social ministry as integral to your spiritual journey, your community and your lifestyle.

EFFICIENCY experts in a factory were trying to
find ways to help the workers be more productive.
They selected a group of men and women working
on an essembly line and indicated that they would
be making some changes in their work environ-
ment in the next few months in order to see what
would help production.

The first change was to improve the lighting
of the area around the assembly line. Immediately,
production rose. Next, longer break periods in the
morning and afternoon were introduced. The production level stayed high. After that, more conversation was allowed to go on during work. Out-
put remained at the high level. Meanwhile, the
lighting was gradually lessened to the point that it
had been before the experiment. No loss in production.

The experts continued to experiment with
adding or removing various elements of the work
climate. Throughout the time, the work efficiency
remained high regardless of the changes made.
Finally, the planners got together and drew their
conclusions. Apparently, production remained
good as long as the workers knew they were getting so much extra attention from management; it
had very little to do with lights or length of
breaks.

Somewhat surprisingly, the same type of
worker success is sometimes evident at a parish
level. Even in the days of emphasis on lay leadership, often the committee or team in the parish
that has significant attention from the pastor

seems to flourish. Without the full support from the pastor, the group may exist and even provide excellent service. Yet it may find itself not doing all it wants, or losing enthusiasm over what it can do.

This is unfortunate simply because not all pastors are able to give the attention that some groups may desire. Survival, growth, and development of the ministry group, then, must depend on the presence of other survival mechanisms. This last chapter, "Don't Stop Now," is, in part, a survival kit for those on the journey of social ministry. In part, it is a *Triptik* that maps future directions in the spiritual development of those traveling a road of service.

SURVIVAL KIT

Several members of a ministry team in one parish wanted to talk. They indicated that when they had first organized, they did not care if the official leaders of the parish supported them. They had formal approval for their work, and their phone number had been published in the parish bulletin. That was enough for them.

When they talked with me, however, they were angry, and realized it. The anger grew out of frustration. Their ministry was having positive effects on those who needed them, but the group felt alone. They longed for direction from the parish leaders, integration with other aspects of the parish life, and just a reminder that they were a vital part of the church's mission.

In addition to talking with the parish leadership about what it needed, several other suggestions can be made about ways for such a group to survive—without increased anger. Any group, with or without parish support, might find these recommendations helpful.

First of all, the group must remember the power of prayer. The members can easily become so aggravated about lack of support, that they forget they can pray among themselves so that they remain faithful to the promptings of the Spirit, who first called them together. I'm frequently amazed at how easily prayer gets put in the background because of more pressing matters.

Secondly, the group members will find some survival strength as they allow some time for really enjoying one another's company. Groups go through life cycles. There is usually a coming together around a purpose. Then as the work is being done, the different members start to discover each other as persons with interesting histories and backgrounds. The level of affection for each other grows. Most groups that I have worked with then arrive at a point when they indicate they want a potluck or picnic with each other.

That's good but not quite enough. The socializing must not all be focused on one day; that is a heavy burden for any 24-hour period. Time for chatting with each other after the work is done is extremely important even when the topic of discussion has little to do with social ministry.

Expectations differ among members. Those who look to the social ministry group to satisfy all their interpersonal needs will be disappointed. Coming together for fun does not mean that the other members must be one's best, or only, friends. There must remain a deep consciousness that all members have their own lives. So while there is to be sharing and play, there has to be great respect of each person's ability to respond.

That leads into the third recommendation—namely, create an internal concern for the other members of the ministry group, much like the service to other hurting men and women of the community. Ministering to fellow ministers may even mean allowing someone to be absent for a while if necessary.

All members of the social ministry group, or any other parish committee, must struggle in balancing the demands of the ministry, their jobs and their families. There is a tension between what one wants to do and what must be done. Again, the reminder for Lone Rangers to work within partnerships or teams can help tremendously. A good team member can be attentive to the other person's struggle and perhaps pick up part of the burden when the other is staggering.

No group survives when it becomes closed. Unfortunately, almost no one admits to being closed. A team of five older men repeatedly told the parish that they wanted some new and younger blood to help them in their work of charity. A couple of women offered to help, indicating that they had some time and a desire to visit the needy. One of the original members, the same one who had asked for help, responded, "But you are not going to be much help to us moving furniture, are you?"

Openness to new members means openness to fresh ideas and different skills. If the ones who are crying out for help simply want someone else made in their own image and likeness, then they will surely go through a great struggle or eventually disintegrate.

Finally, chances for survival are improved when anyone in any type of ministry becomes a coalition builder. If there is a desire to work with other organizations within the parish, or other agencies in the city or county, then there will be a constant source for consultation and help. Some Catholic social services offices in the country have made a special ministry out of trying to "partner" with parish ministry teams. They offer to provide consultation or take referrals, allowing the men and women in the parish who are closest to the need to be the first to administer the love of Christ.

Admittedly, the very notion of suggesting this survival kit is disenchanting to some. Merely surviving sounds like a reduction to the minimal acceptable level. They argue that they don't want simply to survive in their ministry, but actually to thrive in it. Agreed. Yet, whether it is survival or bearing fruit, the recommendations of playing, praying and ministering to one another as well as serving outsiders are still valid guidelines for success.

DIRECTIONS FOR FUTURE TRAVELS

I have always marveled at how many people can read the Surgeon General's warning on a pack of cigarettes as they light up. Somehow, the "dangerous to your health" is not a great deterrent for everyone. Perhaps it even seems a little inviting for younger people who want to take risks.

In the same vein, this final word about social ministry is a type of warning or invitation— whichever way you wish to take it. The warning is that working with the needy will probably start to make you reassess your own values. The invitation is that that assessment may be just what is needed to continue to follow more fully the person of Jesus.

I am not sure which came first for me, the desire to serve the hurting people and the wounded members of the human family, or the attraction to a change of lifestyle. They tend to go together. The alteration of lifestyle may be a radical departure for some. For others, it is an affirmation of the growth that has already been taking place. The lifestyle change will go hand in hand with a drive for a deeper communion with the Lord and a renewed awareness of community.

Moving to a lifestyle built around simplicity can be quite difficult. Because we live in a world of business dealings, finances, and planning for the future, the "consider-the-lilies-of-the-field" approach seems so impractical. Laity, without vows of poverty, may be even more conscious of the tremendous tension between a simple life and the drive toward society's standards for success. This very tension may become the fertile soil for spiritual growth.

Work with needy people, especially with those who are handicapped or economically poor, can be an indicator of what is necessary and what isn't. There is clutter we still hang on to despite our growing unhappiness with the vast amount of space it occupies in our lives. Sometimes the clutter is even that which was purchased for a holy purpose. For me, it is my collection of books. I always want to hang onto them because I may have need for one of them at some time.

A simple lifestyle reflects a conscious choice about the use of time. Playing and praying are both important. However, for the openhearted person there is a generosity connected with his or her availability. A friend of mine, a Franciscan sister, has provided social service for many years at a children's home. Often phone calls come in for crisis care at any time of the day or night. This sister's response is consistent and loving. Although she gets tired and takes her days away like the rest of the staff—she is not a super-woman—non-possessiveness of her own time is a witness of her whole life.

The warning does not read that all those who start to work with the needy will end up with a vow of poverty. Those who reflect on their ministry of service, however, will likely find discontent with being controlled by the possessions they have.

In addition to a drive toward a less materialistic life, the social minister will likely find a need to develop what I call a contemplative stance. This is a profound consciousness of the workings of the Lord in his or her life. A thirst for some silent moments spent with the Creator of the universe will be matched by a hunger for carrying out the Lord's will.

Some excellent books are available today that explain that contemplation is not restricted to the mystics. (The works of Thomas Green, S.J., and William McNamara, O.C.D., are fine examples.) Nevertheless, the understanding of contemplation and the way in which it ties in with a life of service should be highlighted.

Contemplation is a prayer of presence, a prayer of listening. Perhaps it can be called non-active, at least, non-active in our usual busy sense of prayer. Contemplation is spending time with Jesus, already present within each of us, and consciously noting the plan that he unfolds within our lives. Just as Jesus spent time alone in prayer, the person with the busy life needs to go apart once in a while. Admittedly, the time apart may have to be brief, but it can still be sufficient and important.

The contemplative stance, as I call it, is a whole life built around this awareness of the Lord's movings within our lives and our world. It was a day of delightful discovery when I first sat down to read about the great contemplatives of the Christian tradition. I have discovered that these men and women were not removing themselves from the world as they prayed. Their time with the Lord created an acute consciousness of the pains and brokenness of all creation. Thus, a contemplative stance does not turn one off to the reality of the world. Instead it offers hope and promise to that world which the Lord has redeemed.

When someone begins to become active in social ministry, that very service draws him to reflect on it with the Lord. This reflection is the beginning opportunity for contemplation. The further awareness of the mind of God in this quiet prayer hurls the social minister right back into his or her work with renewed conviction that this is the Lord's calling. It is cyclical in that their work leads the social ministers to pray, which in turn directs them back to more work of healing.

Finally, just as values begin to change and contemplation flows from and into a ministry of service, there is also a growing appreciation for community. Perhaps the word community is the most overused word in church circles in the last

20 years. However, the concept should not be avoided. Prayer and service lead one to be fully human, and part of humanity is to be in relationship with others. This relationship is the cornerstone of community.

Evelyn and James Whitehead, in *Community of Faith*, remind their readers that community is neither a loose association with acquaintances at one end of the spectrum nor an intimate friendship at the other. In a community, there is indeed a coming together with some type of concern for each other. Furthermore, the members have a common purpose and some like values. For those involved in social ministry the common purpose is to implement the gospel mandate of love, and the values include a desire to serve the Lord in this work. Thus a community can develop that leads toward the Lord through service to others. This community becomes a practice ground for charity and an impetus for spreading God's love to the entire world. Thus the individual in social ministry finds a special attraction toward community.

During 1983, the internationally active Society of St. Vincent de Paul celebrated its 150th anniversary. What was started by a college student in Paris has survived and become a mainstay in the world of charity and justice. Similarly, during the same year, the Catholic Worker movement, begun by Dorothy Day and Peter Maurin, had its 50th birthday.

Anyone who has worked with the needy must

admire the strengths of associations that can last
so long. Within both the Catholic Worker and St.
Vincent de Paul are individuals who have remained committed for decades.

Will the newly emerging group of social
ministers have the same longevity? Presently there
is profound interest in working with the needy
because of high unemployment and growing social
awareness. A final goal, then, for all those involved in this special work, must be to prevent it
from becoming an ecclesiastical fad that fades by
next year. Seeing social ministry as integrated into
the spiritual journey and linked with communal
development and a lifestyle of detachment may be
the way in which a person can remember not to
stop when this book stops, but to continue in the
ministry that has been begun.